Herbert Puchta and Günter Gerngross

Illustrated by Stefano Misesti

1 **Look and draw lines. Listen and point.**

A living room
B kitchen
C bedroom
D bathroom
E stairs
F garden

2 **Where are the people? Look and draw lines.**

A

B

C

D

E

F

3 **Listen and point.**

This is Daniel. He's ten.
And this is his house and family.
It's Saturday morning. What are
the family doing?
Mum's working in the garden.
Dad's cooking in the kitchen.
Daniel's got a big sister, Ruby.
She's doing her homework.
And what's Daniel doing?
He's playing computer games.

SPEAK

Do you like computer games?
What games do you like?

It's lunchtime.

Can you help in the kitchen, Daniel?

Sorry, Dad, I'm busy. I can't stop my game now.

THINK

Is Daniel's dad happy? Tick (✓).

It's Saturday afternoon.
Dad's washing the dishes. Ruby's helping him. Mum's working in the garden again. And what's Daniel doing? He's playing computer games!

Can you feed the cat, Daniel?

Sorry, Mum, I'm busy. I can't stop my game now!

9

It's Saturday evening. Mum and Dad and Ruby are in the living room. They're laying the table for dinner.

Daniel, can you take the rubbish out?

Sorry, Ruby, I'm busy. I can't stop my game now!

THINK
What is the rubbish?

11

It's Saturday night.
Mum, Dad and Ruby are
going to bed. Daniel's still
playing computer games.

What can
we do?

I've got
an idea...

That's
a great idea!

THINK

What is Ruby's idea?

13

It's Sunday morning.
Daniel and Dad are in the living room.
Dad's reading the paper. Daniel's
looking for a charger for his controller.

Can you help
me, Dad?
I can't find
my charger.

Sorry, Daniel. I'm busy. I'm reading the newspaper.

THINK
Does Dad want to help Daniel?

15

It's Sunday afternoon.
Daniel and Ruby are in their bedroom.
Ruby's reading a book. Daniel's doing
his homework.

Ruby,
can you help
me with my
homework?

Sorry, Daniel. I'm busy. I'm reading a book.

TELL
A FRIEND
What are they doing?

17

It's Sunday evening. Daniel and Mum are in the living room. Mum's working on her laptop. Daniel's looking for his football boots.

Can you help me, Mum? I've got football practice tomorrow. And I can't find my boots!

LOOK

What is the cat doing?

It's Monday afternoon.
Daniel's at football practice. He's wearing his football kit, but not his boots. Everyone's playing football. But Daniel isn't playing.
He hasn't got his boots.
He's thinking.

THINK

What is Daniel thinking?

21

It's Monday evening.
Mum, Dad, Ruby and Daniel are in the kitchen. They are having dinner together.

OK, Daniel!

I'm sorry, Mum, Dad and Ruby. I CAN stop playing computer games when you need me.

CHECK

Look at page 21. Is your guess correct?

23

1 **Put the sentences in order from 1 to 6.**

Sorry, Dad, I'm busy. I can't stop my game now!

Can you feed the cat, Daniel?

Sorry, Mum, I'm busy. I can't stop my game now!

Can you help in the kitchen, Daniel?

Sorry, Ruby, I'm busy. I can't stop my game now!

Daniel, can you take the rubbish out?

2 **Make groups of four. Act the story.**

3 **Write the words.**

Daniel is my ....

Ruby is my ....

brother
sister
son
daughter

Ruby is my ....

Daniel is my ....

4 **Read then write the names.**

Tom is Daniel's friend.
Here is his family.
Suri is Tom's sister.
Jack is Suri's dad.
Tom's mum is Kayla.

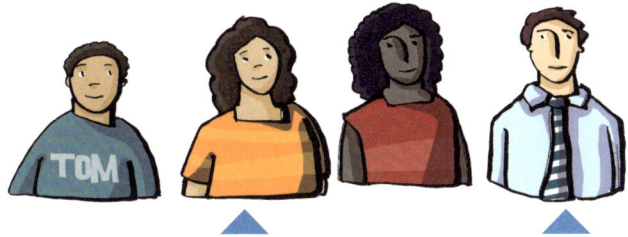

....

....

5 **Think. Write the words.**

Tom is Suri's ....

Kayla is Suri's .... Jack is Tom's ....

25

6   Find 10 differences between the rooms. Point then tell a friend.

7   **Where is the cat? Ask and answer with a friend.**

behind
in front
on
next to

8   **Listen and point.**

9 Listen and draw. Colour the room.

 armchair
 TV
 mirror
lamp
picture

 coffee table
 rug
 sofa
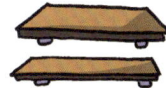 shelves

10 Where do you do these things? Draw lines then tell a friend.

A cook

B watch TV

C have a
shower

D sleep

E read a book

F cut vegetables

G get dressed

H clean your teeth

I wash the dishes

J have a bath

11 **Listen and point.**

My bedroom

Design your perfect bedroom.

You need:

colouring
pencils

glue

scissors

1 Download the pictures from **The Thinking Train** website.

2 Carefully cut out the pictures.

3 Colour them.

4 Stick them onto the bedroom.

5 Describe your perfect bedroom to a friend.